Eyes of Hope

W. Wayne B.

Contains selections from the eBooks Poems: Hope and Love
and Journey Through a Garden

ISBN: 0986097705
ISBN-13: 978-0-9860977-0-6

Dedication

For my parents

Contents

A Source of Hope 9

Summer Fades 10

Pen and Paper..11

Guidance..12

Long Ago 13

The Path 14

The Woods..15

This Moment in Time..16

Today's Picture 17

A New Creation...18

A Mountain Journey 19

The Season of the Year 20

Her Love..21

Flowering Trees 22

Alone 23

The Light of Peace 24

Hope and Joy 25

To the Spirits..26

The People Smile..27

Growth..28

An Afternoon Storm 29

This Road 30

Someone Else 31

Beauty..32

Secure Together..33

Walking Through 34

A Beautiful Day 35

To My Friends 36

My Voice..37

My Soul is Lost 38

Along the Beach 39

That Beautiful Garden....................................40

I Look Inside..41

This Morning of Life 42

A New Home..43

Tomorrow Will Change 44

Companions 45

The Rising Sun...46

Gems 47

Late 48

On The Shore Of The Lake 49

Signs of My Love...50

Army of Light 51

Share My Love 52

Pursuit...53

Beyond 54

Journeying...55

Acknowledgements

I'm grateful for the support of my friend Erik for encouraging me to keep going. Also Todd for his enthusiasm at the upcoming finishing of the book. My sister Nancy for our interesting conversations about history and the use of technology in research. My sisters Diane and Sue helped me by reading early versions of this book.

I'm especially grateful for my parents and their support through good times and bad. They kept me moving forward when everything seemed to be falling down.

A Source of Hope

Tomorrow will not come soon enough.

I am waiting to journey away.
Can I bring along a source of hope?

What can I do alone?
I am lost in this silent moment.
The names in my heart do not fade.

I will begin a new adventure soon.
I will journey through the worlds.
Even my soul will travel a new path.
I wait with a smile for the new creation.

Summer Fades

I am sitting near the fountain again.

I see leaves fall before me as summer fades.

The water's whispers sooth me.

Why don't I come here more often?

The leaves are almost gone.

Clouds fill the sky with gray shadows.

I am joyful today—my life is complete.

Soon the fountain will stop.

The water will drain away.

When Spring returns, I will find joy again.

Pen and Paper

To trace the outline of my life,
I use a simple pen and paper.
Sometimes I use colors.
Sometimes black is good enough.

Usually, I cannot share my insights.
My thoughts are deep and personal.
However, I grow stronger each time I draw.

I did not find the door into my heart alone.
I emulate the experiences of my predecessors.
When they make a suggestion,
I listen to their guidance with care.

I long to live as if I were a butterfly.
I could be carried away on the wind.
As I come close to flowers,
I would be filled with love.
The aroma of the petals would lift me up.
I would land softly and enjoy the day.

Guidance

The sun fills my life with love.

Her shining glow helps me heal.

I see the breeze dispel the mist.

I will not live my life so far away.

I had been in the middle of a life of pain.

Yet, my heart has found hope here.

Although we are far apart today,

I look to you for an answer.

As I weep, I hear your voice.

I am growing stronger now.

I try to walk the direct path.

I am listening to your guidance.

Today, we can pass by the dawn together.

Long Ago

Long ago, the trees took root.

The sun gave them life.

Rain quenched their thirst.

Sisters and brothers, they all grew tall.

I was surprised to see their joy.

Now, the field is a happy woodland.

The birds above me

fill the air with life.

The trees add soft whispers

to the cool breezes of Spring.

A white flower grows at my feet.

I am in awe of God's bounty.

The Path

I've been watching the quiet rain.

I am following a difficult road.

Why would I forget the path to safety?

I feel that I don't belong.

I wonder about strange mysteries.

This place is alien and confusing.

I have been planning to go away.

I have lost my home; I have few choices.

I am at the shore of the ocean.

I see seagulls darting here and there.

I want to hope and find a reason.

The sand is wet along the beach.

The world was not made for one like me.

I sink beneath the waves and try to sleep.

A peace flows over me and I rest endlessly.

The Woods

I am walking the road down a rolling hill.
Trees, strong and tall, surround the path.
Oaks, maples and poplars fill the woods.
The forest stretches for miles around me.

I relish the shade the trees provide.
Their glorious beauty fills my heart.
I work my legs on an excursion of hope.

Mud on the road resists my progress.
I step carefully over the streamlets and pools.
I am busy today so I don't play with the water.
I walk the road with a smile on my face.

This Moment in Time

I am staying in the moment.
A song lightens my burden.

I've been working hard today.
Words form on my smiling lips.
My mind is full of light.

Perhaps my story is boring.
I try to keep the tempo up.
I practice hope today.

I am filling my mind with truth.
These words fill my heart with life.

Today's Picture

I am drawing a picture today.
It will show my love for life.

Hopeful colors fill the sky.
The trees are verdant and full of fruit.
The background has snowcapped mountains.
These beauties beckon me to approach.

I am no master and cannot finesse a subtle mood.
My pen is cautious and my hand is timid.

The picture's world will be a mirror of my mind.
I feel full of beauty as I smile.

A New Creation

This is a beautiful day.
The rain falls peacefully.
Trees spread their shade along the street.
The sun will light the sky at sunset.

I imagine the animals crawling in their burrows.
I am listening to the songs of happy birds.
A butterfly passes me slowly.

My mind bursts with a fountain of hope.
Words cannot describe the glow of life.

My gratitude grows in this new creation.

A Mountain Journey

I came to you through the mountains.

They have peaks robed with snow.

Every moment reveals a new vista.

The clouds parted to reveal the sun.

I approached the lake below the glacier.

I saw its silver, mirrored surface.

Birds of prey searched for fish.

As I watched them dive, I felt true freedom.

The Season of the Year

This season is calm and serene.

Today began without a cloud.

I walked through my garden in peace.

My power and energy are growing.

I have many ways to spend my time.

This afternoon has a soothing breeze.

Days go by quickly.

Night falls with beautiful colors.

A floating moon casts a silver sheen.

What a beautiful lake amidst the prairie.

Her Love

I saw her love for me.
It was easy to see her beauty.

I saw what seemed to be a smile.
I felt like I was floating that day.
Images of her have filled my mind.

Yesterday's memories are far away.
Today I wish to learn new truths.

My longing allows me to love her still.
The dreams warm my heart.
I hope she will come home soon.

Flowering Trees

Flowering trees accent the landscape.
It is springtime and their beauty is everywhere.
The bushes are growing; flowerbeds teem with life.
Blossoms appear where there had been mud.

The season is building to a climax.
Every rain shower and each sunny day
gives life and new growth to the park.

After the blossoms have fallen and been forgotten,
fruit will grow in abundance this summer.

The springtime season is one of rebirth.

Alone

My eternal days alone are gone.

I share love with new friends.

My hope grows stronger as I feel it.

I am beginning to feel love.

I find a new challenge when I listen.

How will I shine at the dawn?

Today I walk my path with strength and resolve.

I am finding a new hope.

I had been walking a lonely life of fear.

However, I am not alone in my journey anymore.

The Light of Peace

I see the light of peace grow today.

Words fill me with hope.
Each sentence helps break the darkness.

Soon I will have a new home.
I want to learn how to feel joy.
I am searching for a companion.

The people around me don't understand.
I want the best for my friends.
When I speak, I guard my words.
I often leave my intentions hidden.

As I move through the day,
I learn beautiful new ideas.
I relish the practice they give.
I am an enemy of conflict.
I have begun to heal my life.

Hope and Joy

I feel hope and joy today.

I find truth in those I cherish.

Our journey together sustains me.

As they help me grow, I feel warm.

Our lives are built upon hidden depths.

No one fathoms the lives of my companions.

As we pray, our spirits are nourished.

Our growth is subtle and unseen.

The virtues ripen slowly,

but the fruits are pure.

To the Spirits

To the spirit of the night,

> Protect me from the evil around me.
>
> Help me rest and awaken on time.
>
> Keep me safe from the wrongs I have done.
>
> Be with me until dawn.

To the spirit of the day,

> Guide my hand to help the others.
>
> Show me God's will for this brief span.
>
> Begin my day with a breath of life.
>
> Show me where to turn in joy.

I am grateful for your love.

I do not always see you in my life.

I come closer when I wait with a quiet patience.

Bless me with one more cycle.

Bless me with a gift each day.

The People Smile

I am sitting on a bench in the town's center.
I see people smile as they walk by.

As I rest, I feel a fresh breeze.

The sunlight is filtered by a powerful tree.
Drifting clouds move through the sky.
The shade I enjoy will not last long.

I feel that I am home here.
I talk to a friend about my life.
I grow in peace every day.
The things I need are coming in their own time.

Growth

I am beginning to grow.

Life is not so hard anymore.

I love to share my experiences.

I have walked through an open door.

My heart is at peace.

I give away pure love.

I am not as lost today.

My eyes have started to shine.

I see more love in this new light.

I look ahead and it is enough.

When I am with friends, I am fearless.

I never hide when I am free.

An Afternoon Storm

The storm passed slowly.
The sun set in the clearing western sky.
Then I saw a brilliant rainbow above.

My mood was brightened by the sight.
My heart began to warm.
I forgot the storm's fury.

The sunlight's colors changed.
The trees began to calm slowly.
Peace returned to my garden.

The storm washed my worries from the day.
I no longer felt inferior and helpless.
When tomorrow comes, I will live for that day.

This Road

When I drive along this road,
I see trees flash by the window.

I wonder who will open the door.

Our house is the same gray blue.
The landscaping is impeccable.
When I step inside, I will smell the spiced candle.
I know that they love me as always.

We are not a perfect family.
However, because we are trying,
our love increases even more.

Someone Else

Truly I have only briefly been aware:

>—that my friends care for me deeply.

>—that they all wish for me to grow.

>—that they all hope I will feel a part of the world.

I felt I was a social outcast.
Society had nothing to offer me.
No one could understand my life.
I wished that I was someone else.
My growth as a human has been frozen.

My changes have been gradual.
I did not notice that I was different.
The barriers fell as I spent time with friends.
Now I don't feel so broken.

Beauty

I see the morning blossoms fade.

Once they are gone, I will plant their seeds.

I am growing love in the garden of my heart.

As the inner flowers grow,

a soft fragrance fills my spirit.

I strive to fill my life with beauty.

Sometimes words fail me.

I can only weep with gratitude.

I trust the winds of fate.

Time will bring me good fortune.

I have received many gifts in my life.

I have good dreams and steadfast hope.

Now I can enjoy my Lord's bounty.

Secure Together

As the moments pass, I feel secure with you.

The days behind us forged a strong bond.

Our friendship grows stronger each day.

Our memories have built a park.

We have made our perfect garden.

It has paths for others to share.

Its trees give us a shelter through the storms.

Their golden leaves are gifts we share with others.

Our friends play games as we laugh with joy.

Walking Through

I'm walking through a newly planted garden.

The flowers are growing in the rain.

As I see the lights of my home,

I feel joy from my love

for nature. I require

little to make

me happy

today.

A Beautiful Day

What a beautiful day!
The sun fills the sky.
The breeze is fresh and pure.
I like these days of light.

I look up and remember my youth.
I would walk through the fields.
A plow would turn the earth.
In its time, the hay would be cut.

I remember that words are powerful.
Each syllable can bring back memories.
I listen to the birds above me.
Their tunes are bright and full of joy.

A small animal runs by.
I laugh as it climbs a tree.
It reached the crown in moments.
I don't think it saw me as is escaped.

What do I need to hear today?
The breeze tousles my hair.
I expect that it will be cold soon.
What a beautiful day!

To My Friends

I am speaking to my beloved friends.
I have found a new path.

The darkness that filled my spirit is gone.
A glowing star shines there now.

I look back on the days before.
All I see is black fear stalking me.

My story was full of hopelessness.
The road ahead, lost in the night.

Now I have discovered new eyes of hope.
Your love showed me the way.

Thank you.

My Voice

I have found my voice again today.

The words I speak feel like magic.
I see their waves spread around me.

In the whispers of a breeze,
my inner light flickers like a torch.
When I am silent, my spirit is full of peace.

As I speak to a friend today,
my words are gentle and uplifting.
Everyone I meet is a mirror.
In my reflection, I see that I am not alone.

My fears come and go as I breathe.
Sometimes I restrain my words.
I allow the world to pass me peacefully.
When I allow myself to speak,
I am kind because I care so much.

My Soul is Lost

My soul is lost in its love for you.

To share that love, my heart shines bright.

Its inner light longs for a path.

A few short words rush to its aid.

Their powerful eyes search for a trail.

Five fingers call for they know the way.

A pen listens with yearning to explain these words.

The ink calls out so the brightness can spread.

The ink, pen, fingers, words, light and heart

all dance together with my love for you.

Along the Beach

I travel from a shore of joy

        into an ocean of ecstasy.

Countless grains of sand meet

        endless drops of water.

I walk along the beach.

When I jump into the surf,

        the foam grows thick.

Can you come with me while the day is young?

I will share my love with you.

We can progress together through every storm.

That Beautiful Garden

I walked through that beautiful garden.

My eyes were filled with flowing colors.

The garden's purity overwhelmed my senses.

Once I returned home, I was sad.

I brought back no mementos.

No stem, no blossom, not even a photo.

Tomorrow I will return to the garden.

I hope to visit an uncharted corner.

I have never seen such fields of green.

I honor the creators of the garden.

They have filled it with perfect life.

I know they care for it with love and power.

I Look Inside

I look inside my heart with care.
I find an attitude of love and hope.
With every positive thought, I grow stronger.

I hope to meet you soon.
Our time together is coming near.
I want to share my path with you.

I light a small lamp at my side.
In the warm glow, I overcome the cold.
Darkness is defeated by my shimmering candle.

I want the world to be a home for us both.
We will be together again.
Love beats in our hearts together.
With a rhythm of strength we shine.

This Morning of Life

I wake to see the morning flourish.
Unsurpassed beauty fills my eyes again.

The sun shines with unrestrained joy.
The sky loves the glory and plays its part.
The splendor of dawn is an irresistible force.

My heart no longer is a slave of darkness.
My nights of bleak silence are gone.
Now I fill my home with light.
Each sunrise inspires my spirit.

Now I am alive and treasure each day.

A New Home

This morning I ran to my new home.
I caught the smile of a friend.
He was laughing and full of joy.

I am not familiar with this place.
I used to live hours from here.
I am far from you again.
Have I left our love behind?

Although I remember amber maples,
they are a beauty lost to time.
Outside my window is a cherry tree.
I look forward to its glorious petals.
Spring will renew its branches.

I don't need to run any more.
I am at peace and look forward to resting.

I hope that it will all be ok.

Tomorrow Will Change

When I sing, my voice is pure and sweet.

I grow happier as the song rises.

The words I chant are smooth and round.

I sing with tones that climb to the sky.

I see that today is different from yesterday.

Tomorrow will change yet more.

Days come and go as if they were moments.

I'd love to seek out the future.

I'm too attached to the present for that.

I will wait a little longer for it to arrive.

Companions

When I walk through the woods,
I see the trees falling and hear nothing.
When I walk through the city,
I see nothing and hear the city falling.

The world turns with immense force.
The changing sky is over us all.
I see beauty in every sunset.

My plans change each day.
My plans for the tomorrow are tenuous.

I am in a garden, looking for companions.

The Rising Sun

Today, I watched the sunrise.
I remembered a dawn from long ago.
The fading moon has fled the sky again.

My eyes reviewed the celestial dome.
The sky is always beautiful.
As a bird called, I looked up.
The eagle crossed the lake in freedom.

It is rare that I wake up so early.

When I see the morning begin,
the day is special and I am full of joy.

Gems

The princess of truth found diamonds and rubies.

She gathered all the gems she could find.

She scattered the stones to the wind.

Now their beauty did not matter.

They were lost in mud and barren thickets.

Some fell in weeds and a few were among roses.

The King found the gems and rescued them.

He did not regard their resting place.

He polished them carefully and ignited their fire.

The spirit of each of us hides a hidden treasure.

When the One finds a home for that bounty,

the jewel's value will fulfill its promise.

Late

In the late blooming morning
Around the tree by the road
Under the shining sun

Listening to words of love
Finding the power around me
Resting in giant caring arms

Together under a perfect sky
Watching the golden sun go down
Seeing hope in the eyes of a friend

Communing softly in prayer
Finding companionship together
Sighing as the day ends again

On The Shore Of The Lake

I was standing on the shore of a lake.

I watched waves wash onto the beach.

Birds were calling out.

I saw fish breaching the water.

I don't remember the weather that day.

I'm not sure why I was there.

I do know that I felt abundant hope.

My friend returned from his travels.

I am glad for his company.

These pleasant memories still linger.

Signs of My Love

Signs of my love will not be hidden.

It is strange to me that it would be avoided.

Love is like a light shining day and night.

Why would one forsake its beauty?

Hope is very familiar to me.

Renewal of my thoughts is not a surprise.

Why would I hide from a spirit full of life?

What secret could I keep from you?

I will share my heart with you.

I will not deny our special connection.

I will spend my life with you gladly.

I know we will grow closer and closer.

Army of Light

I am surrounded by an army of light.
I hear pure sounds and simple words.
I have found the way of love and joy.

Each person has a meaning that I accept.
They all have a purpose.
They each have formed a plan.

In the moments I share with them, I find beauty.
It is as if I am looking at a perfect rose.
I never see thorns or weeds.

At night, I walk through a vast forest.
A chorus of love fills the air.
Each day I hear the symphony more clearly.

Every word fills my heart with hope.
I feel the songs strengthen me.
I do not fight; I am at peace.

Share My Love

Soon I will be sharing my love.

I speak that truth I know:

> I feel calm.
>
> I feel patient,
>
> I feel free.

My hopes for today are simple:

> A heart that smiles.
>
> A mind at peace.
>
> A spirit full of joy.

Most of the days I'm strong.

In times of weakness, I am protected.

I thank you for each of my gifts.

I am grateful for each moment.

I cannot repay you for the days I live.

Pursuit

Positive of happy pursuits,
the young man forged on:
A goal well within reach.

Frequently, he searched for it.
Desperately, he found nothing.
Hopeful, he still remained.
Quietly, he found a solution.

A goal well within reach,
the young man forged on:
Positive of happy pursuits.

Beyond

Beyond the canopy of stars,
farther than the galaxies and clouds of dust,
there is a mysterious place
where love plants hidden seeds.

The growth of their flowers
is astounding, fragrant and pure.
The phases of love reward
the small effort to plant the seed.

I am lucky to be the one
who danced in the garden.
Faith grows strong when fed
with hope, love and trust.

Journeying

In transit from the world

Escaping the bonds of time
Approaching a shelter of strength

Amazed by the lights of glory
Watching the border approach
Seeing a friend arrive to greet me

Briefly alone in a vast corridor
Silently moving on
Looking ahead full of hope

Lifting my eyes to the sky
Resting in the arms of love

Closing the book's first volume

www.ingramcontent.com/pod-product-compliance
Lightning Source LLC
Chambersburg PA
CBHW060617030426
42337CB00018B/3098